A WHO HQ GRAPHIC NOVEL

Who Was the Girl Warrior of France?

JOAN OF ARC

D0100899

by Sarah Winifred Searle
illustrated by Maria Capelle Frantz

Penguin Workshop

Introduction

Joan of Arc is the English name for a girl from France whose first name was "Jeanne" and whose last name was "d'Arc"—Jeanne d'Arc in French.

Jeanne d'Arc took a deep breath of cold January air while she finished helping her father, Jacques, and three brothers with the early morning farm chores one last time. Jeanne's sister and her mother, Isabelle, greeted them with wooden bowls of hot porridge as they hurried back inside to sit around the fireplace. Jeanne took a minute from her breakfast to appreciate how cozy this house felt when filled with her family and their voices. She was going to miss this warmth.

Jeanne was nervous—today, she was leaving home in Domrémy for the town of Vaucouleurs. She was only sixteen years old, but God's angels had been visiting her through visions since she was thirteen. The angels—Saint Michael, Saint Catherine, and Saint Margaret—spoke to her through the shifting light of her church's candles, the whistle of the wind, and the ache in her heart when she thought about the war that was happening around her. They revealed God's mission for her: Heaven chose Jeanne, also known as Joan of Arc, to end the Hundred Years' War and lead France to freedom.

The mission felt huge. The war had been raging on and off

for about ninety years and was destroying Jeanne's country, including her village. She had to tell the heir to the French throne, the dauphin, of her visions. But in order to get to the dauphin in faraway Chinon, she needed permission from Robert de Baudricourt to travel there. As lord of her region and commander of the fort in Vaucouleurs, he was the only person who had the swords, the men, and the horses to get her there safely.

In fact, she had visited Vaucouleurs once before to ask Lord Baudricourt for help, and he had said no. But that wasn't going to stop her this time.

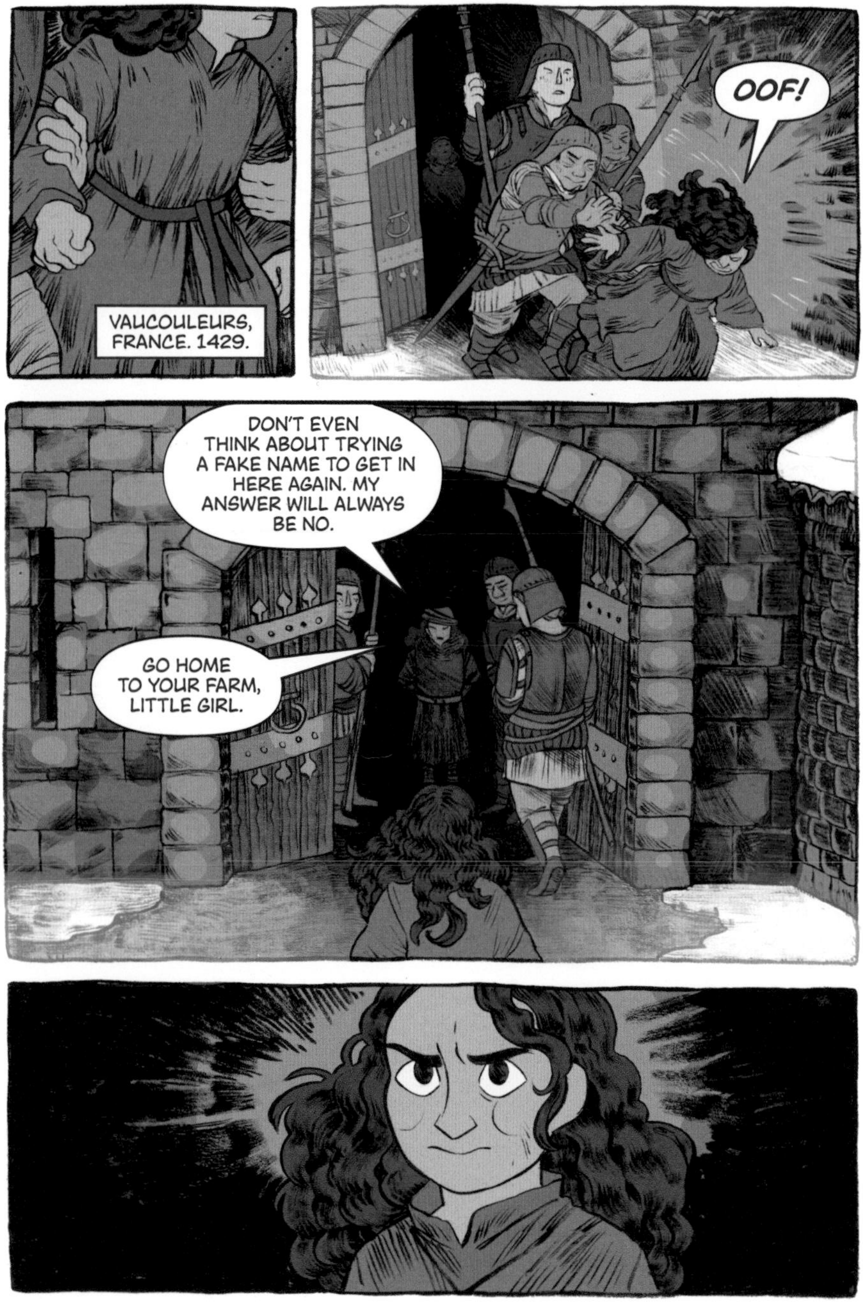
VAUCOULEURS, FRANCE. 1429.
OOF!
DON'T EVEN THINK ABOUT TRYING A FAKE NAME TO GET IN HERE AGAIN. MY ANSWER WILL ALWAYS BE NO.
GO HOME TO YOUR FARM, LITTLE GIRL.

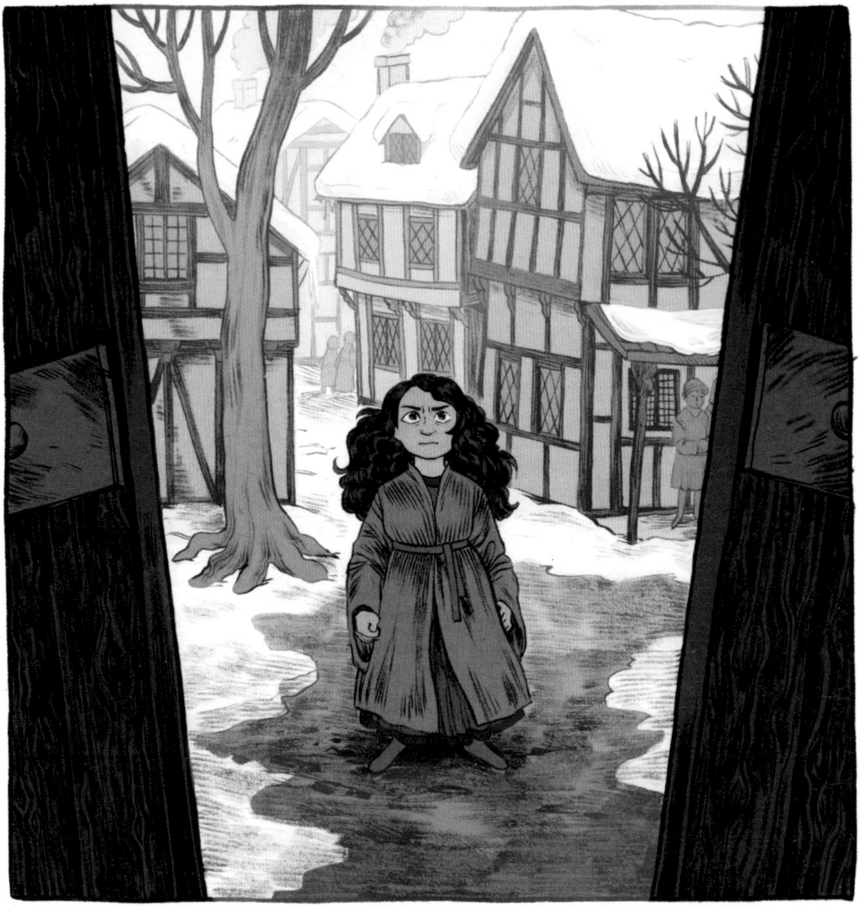

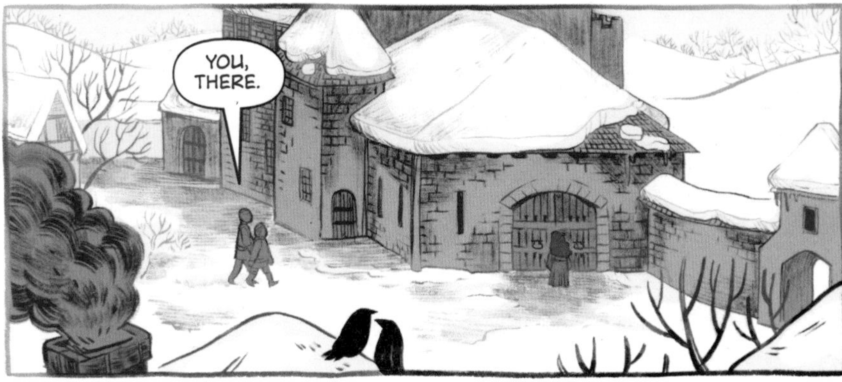
YOU, THERE.

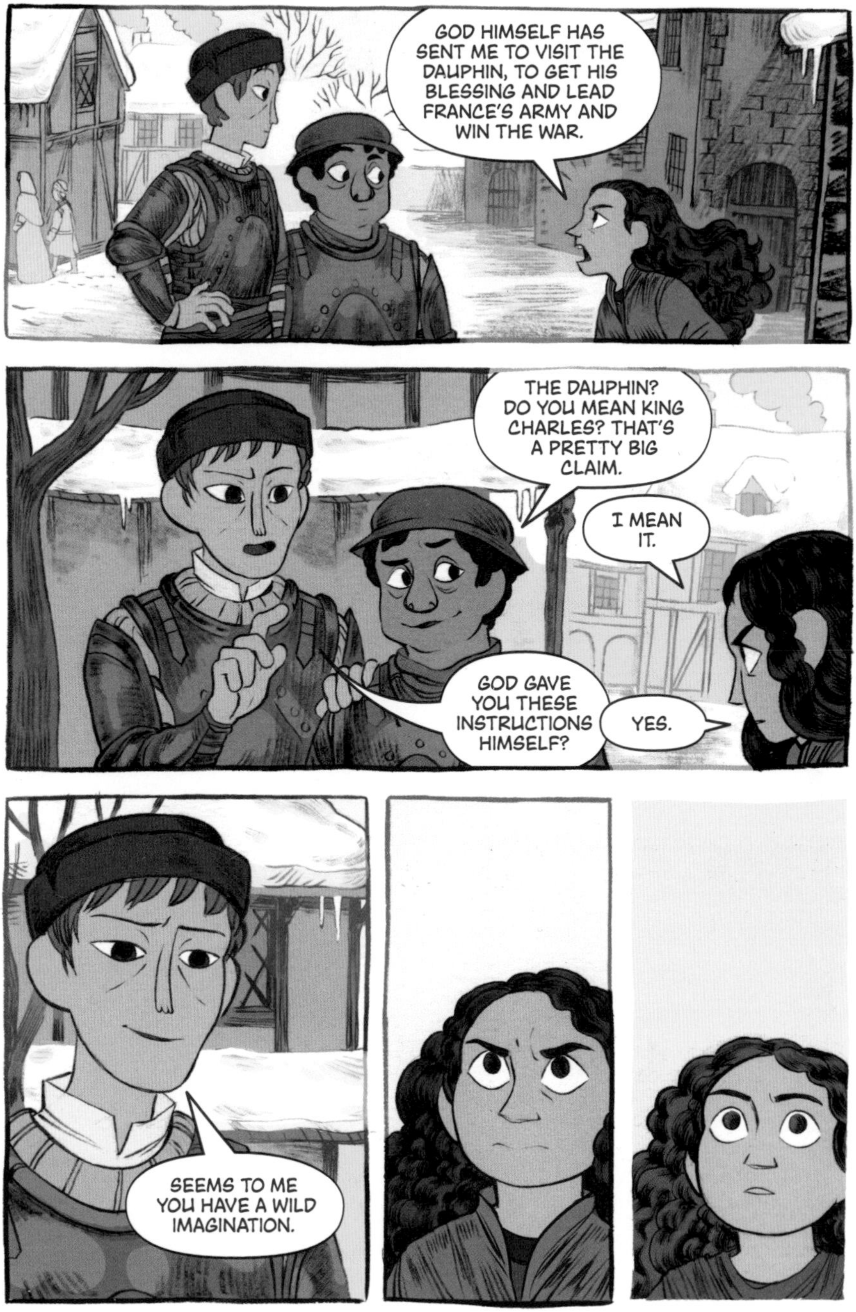
GOD HIMSELF HAS SENT ME TO VISIT THE DAUPHIN, TO GET HIS BLESSING AND LEAD FRANCE'S ARMY AND WIN THE WAR.
THE DAUPHIN? DO YOU MEAN KING CHARLES? THAT'S A PRETTY BIG CLAIM.
I MEAN IT.
GOD GAVE YOU THESE INSTRUCTIONS HIMSELF?
YES.
SEEMS TO ME YOU HAVE A WILD IMAGINATION.

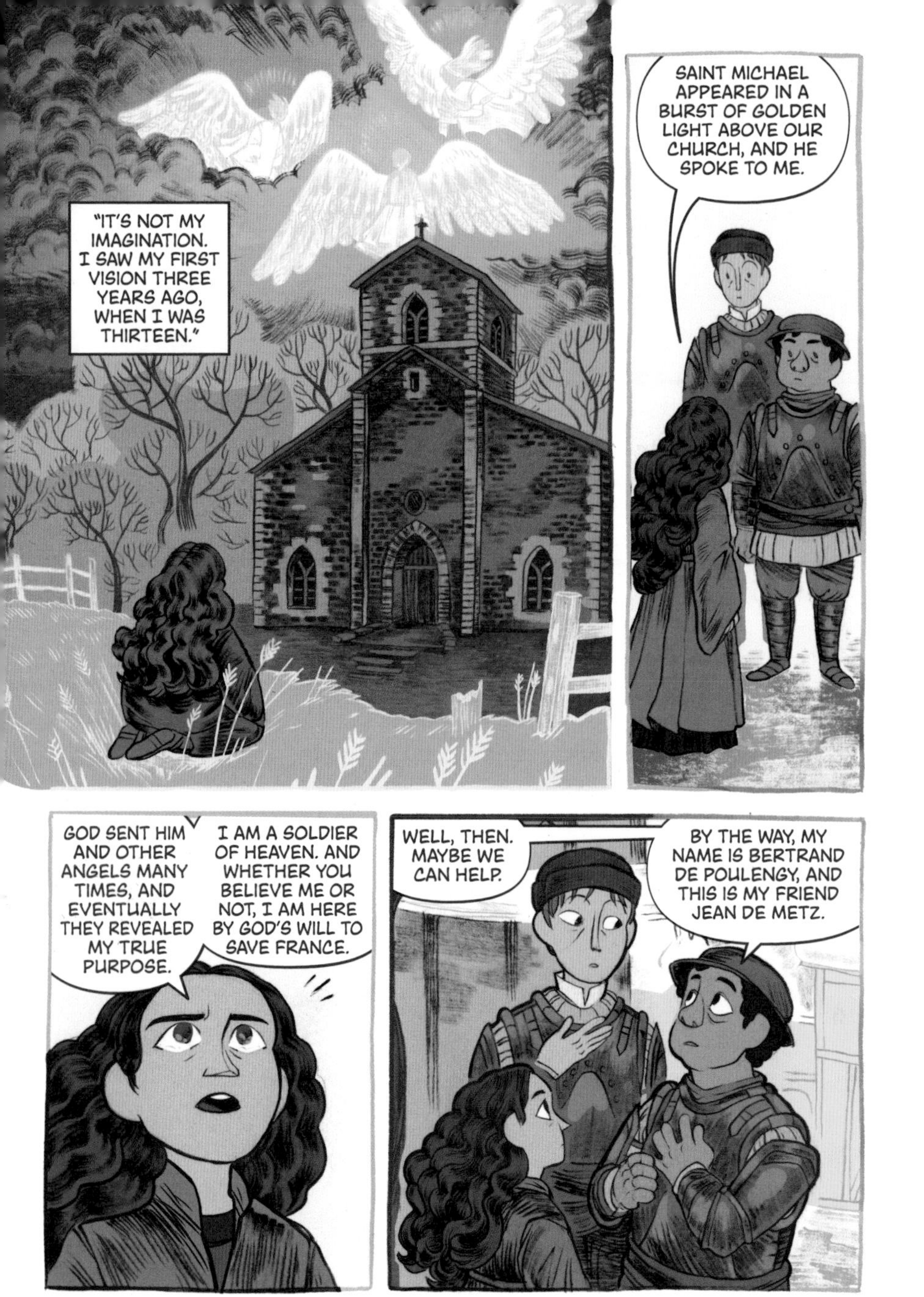
"IT'S NOT MY IMAGINATION. I SAW MY FIRST VISION THREE YEARS AGO, WHEN I WAS THIRTEEN."
SAINT MICHAEL APPEARED IN A BURST OF GOLDEN LIGHT ABOVE OUR CHURCH, AND HE SPOKE TO ME.
GOD SENT HIM AND OTHER ANGELS MANY TIMES, AND EVENTUALLY THEY REVEALED MY TRUE PURPOSE.
I AM A SOLDIER OF HEAVEN. AND WHETHER YOU BELIEVE ME OR NOT, I AM HERE BY GOD'S WILL TO SAVE FRANCE.
WELL, THEN. MAYBE WE CAN HELP.
BY THE WAY, MY NAME IS BERTRAND DE POULENGY, AND THIS IS MY FRIEND JEAN DE METZ.

11

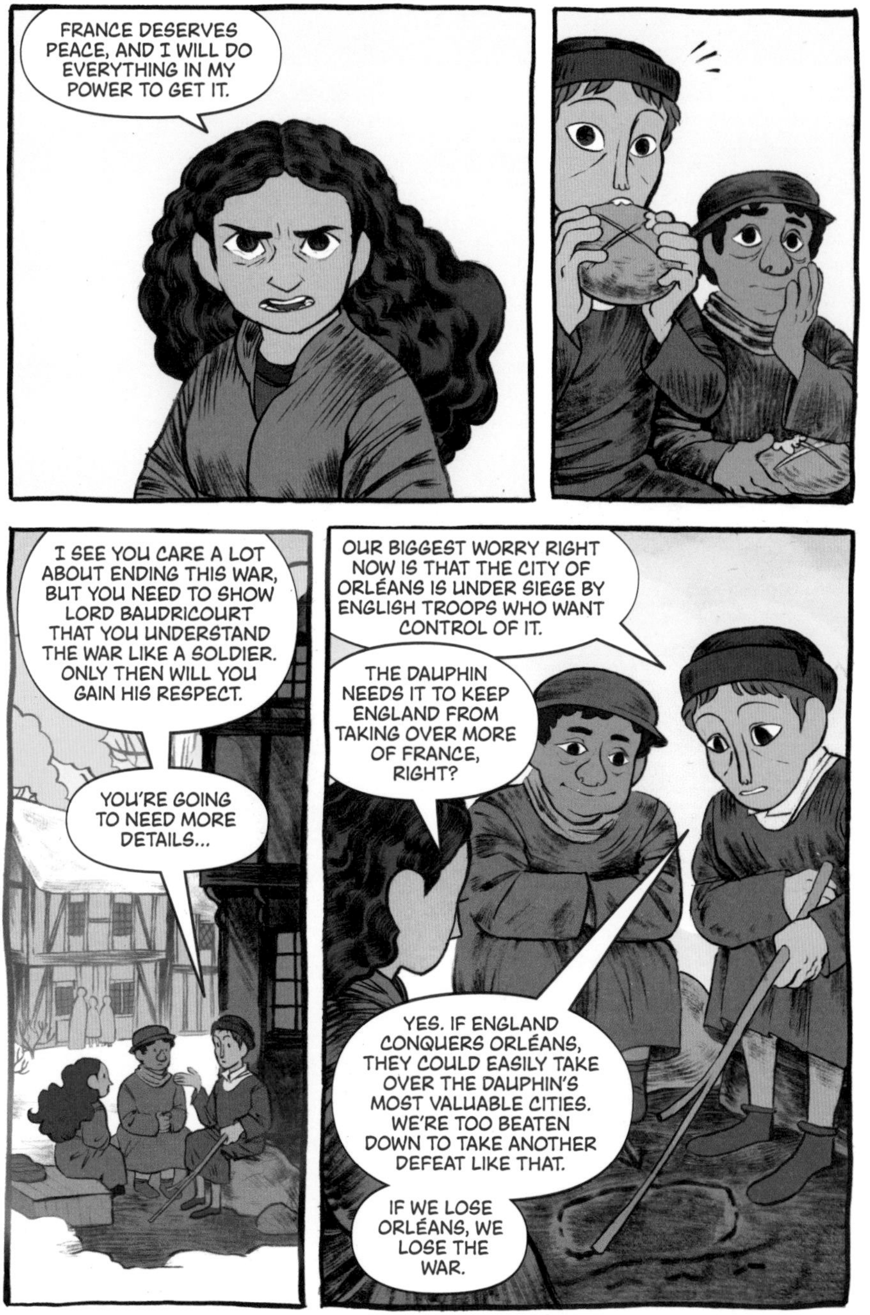
FRANCE DESERVES PEACE, AND I WILL DO EVERYTHING IN MY POWER TO GET IT.
I SEE YOU CARE A LOT ABOUT ENDING THIS WAR, BUT YOU NEED TO SHOW LORD BAUDRICOURT THAT YOU UNDERSTAND THE WAR LIKE A SOLDIER. ONLY THEN WILL YOU GAIN HIS RESPECT.
YOU'RE GOING TO NEED MORE DETAILS...
OUR BIGGEST WORRY RIGHT NOW IS THAT THE CITY OF ORLÉANS IS UNDER SIEGE BY ENGLISH TROOPS WHO WANT CONTROL OF IT.
THE DAUPHIN NEEDS IT TO KEEP ENGLAND FROM TAKING OVER MORE OF FRANCE, RIGHT?
YES. IF ENGLAND CONQUERS ORLÉANS, THEY COULD EASILY TAKE OVER THE DAUPHIN'S MOST VALUABLE CITIES. WE'RE TOO BEATEN DOWN TO TAKE ANOTHER DEFEAT LIKE THAT.
IF WE LOSE ORLÉANS, WE LOSE THE WAR.

The Hundred Years' War

In 1328, King Charles IV of France died. With no sons to inherit the throne, two different royal families soon claimed the right to rule France. King Edward III of England thought he should be king because he was Charles IV's nephew. But France had other plans—they crowned Charles IV's French cousin, King Philip VI, as the rightful heir. To make matters more complicated, Burgundy, France's neighbor to the west, sided with England in the fight.

This began a war that lasted on and off from 1337 to 1453. English and Burgundian soldiers often raided French villages by attacking and killing innocent people and stealing their food and valuables. France's citizens couldn't feel safe with this war that seemed like it would never end.

Over the course of the Hundred Years' War, somewhere between two and three million people died.

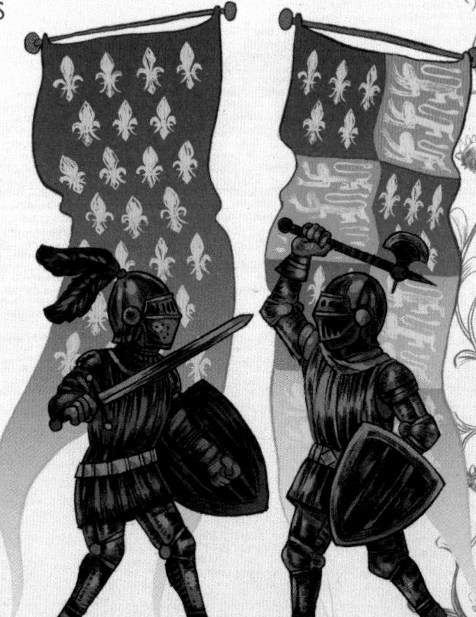

15

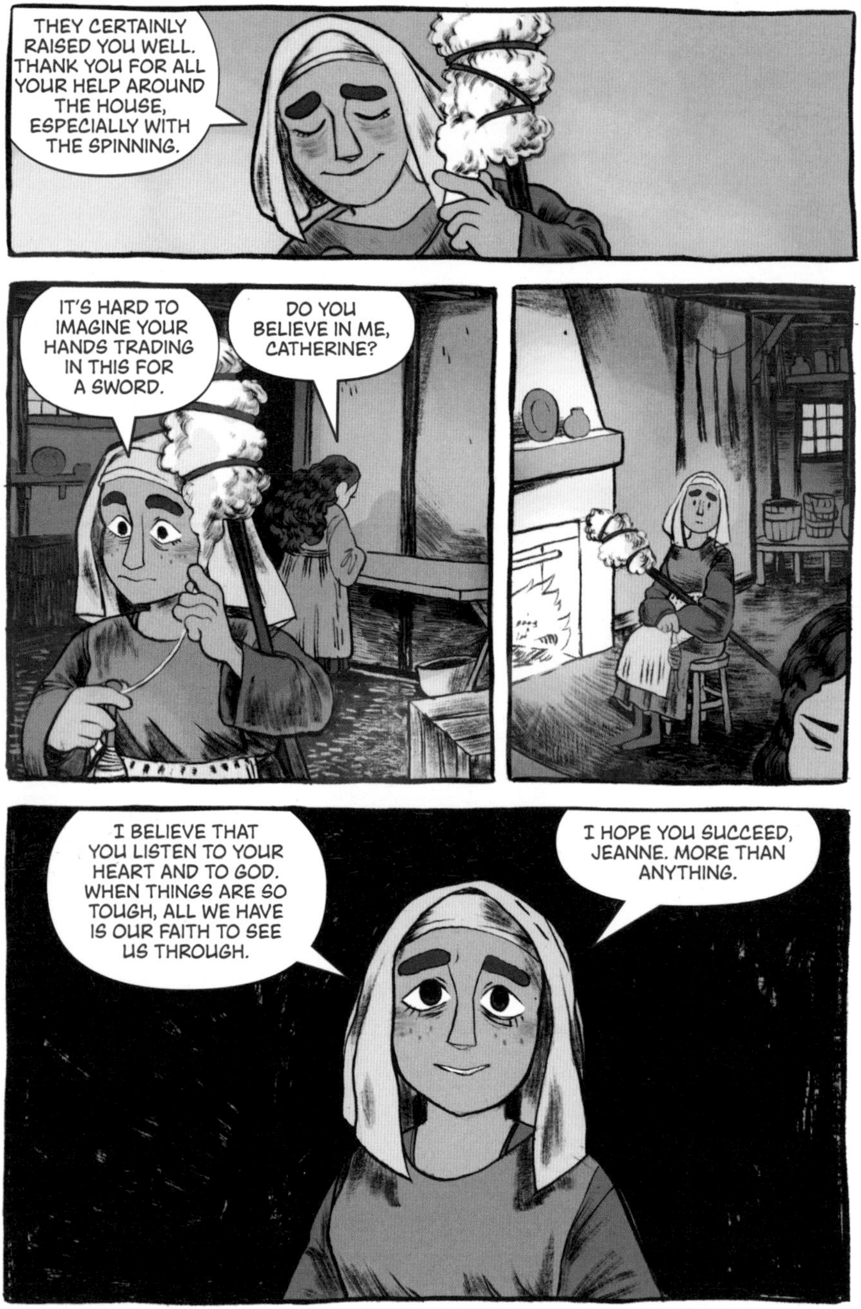
THEY CERTAINLY RAISED YOU WELL. THANK YOU FOR ALL YOUR HELP AROUND THE HOUSE, ESPECIALLY WITH THE SPINNING.
IT'S HARD TO IMAGINE YOUR HANDS TRADING IN THIS FOR A SWORD.
DO YOU BELIEVE IN ME, CATHERINE?
I BELIEVE THAT YOU LISTEN TO YOUR HEART AND TO GOD. WHEN THINGS ARE SO TOUGH, ALL WE HAVE IS OUR FAITH TO SEE US THROUGH.
I HOPE YOU SUCCEED, JEANNE. MORE THAN ANYTHING.

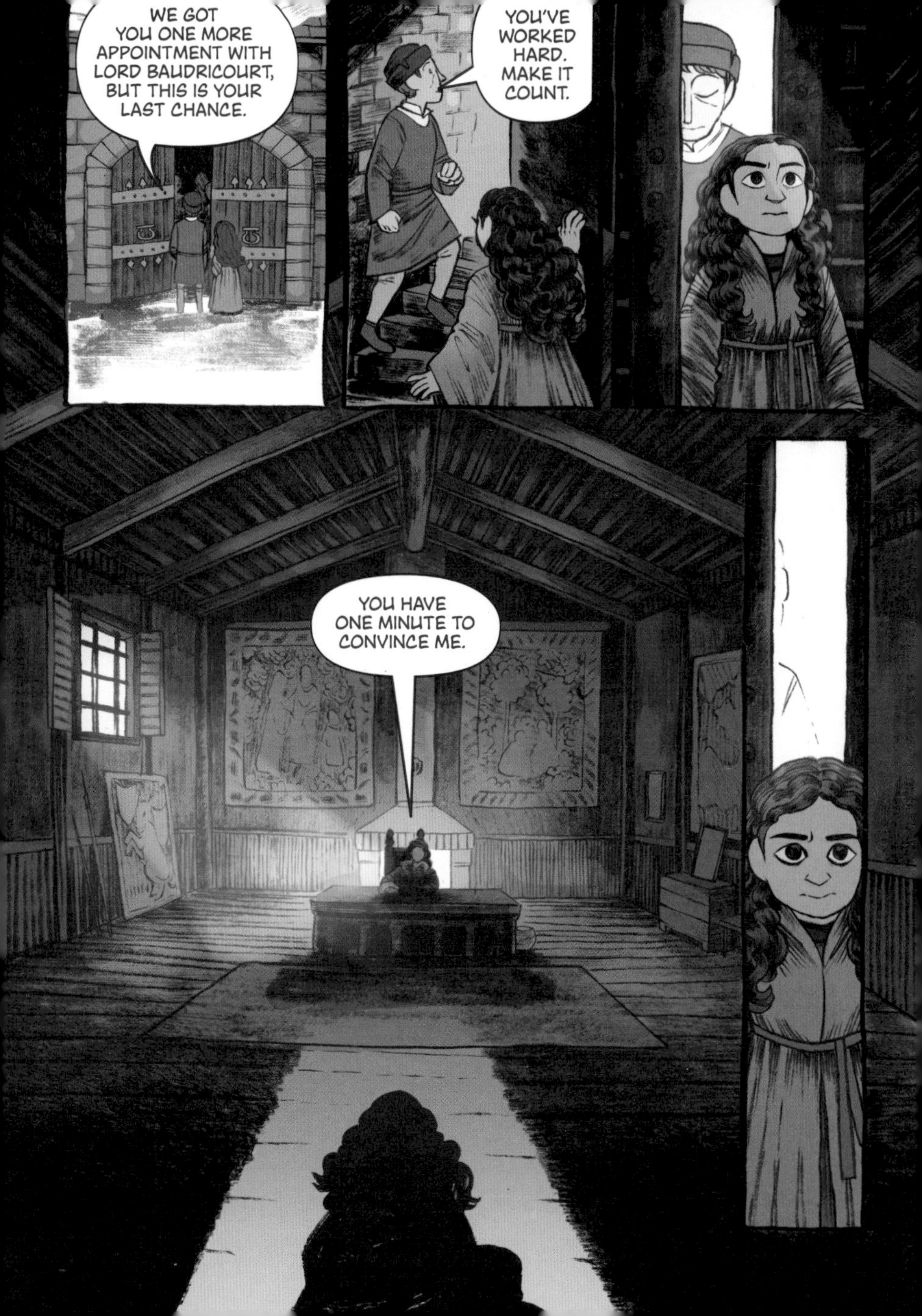
WE GOT YOU ONE MORE APPOINTMENT WITH LORD BAUDRICOURT, BUT THIS IS YOUR LAST CHANCE.
YOU'VE WORKED HARD. MAKE IT COUNT.
YOU HAVE ONE MINUTE TO CONVINCE ME.

21

23

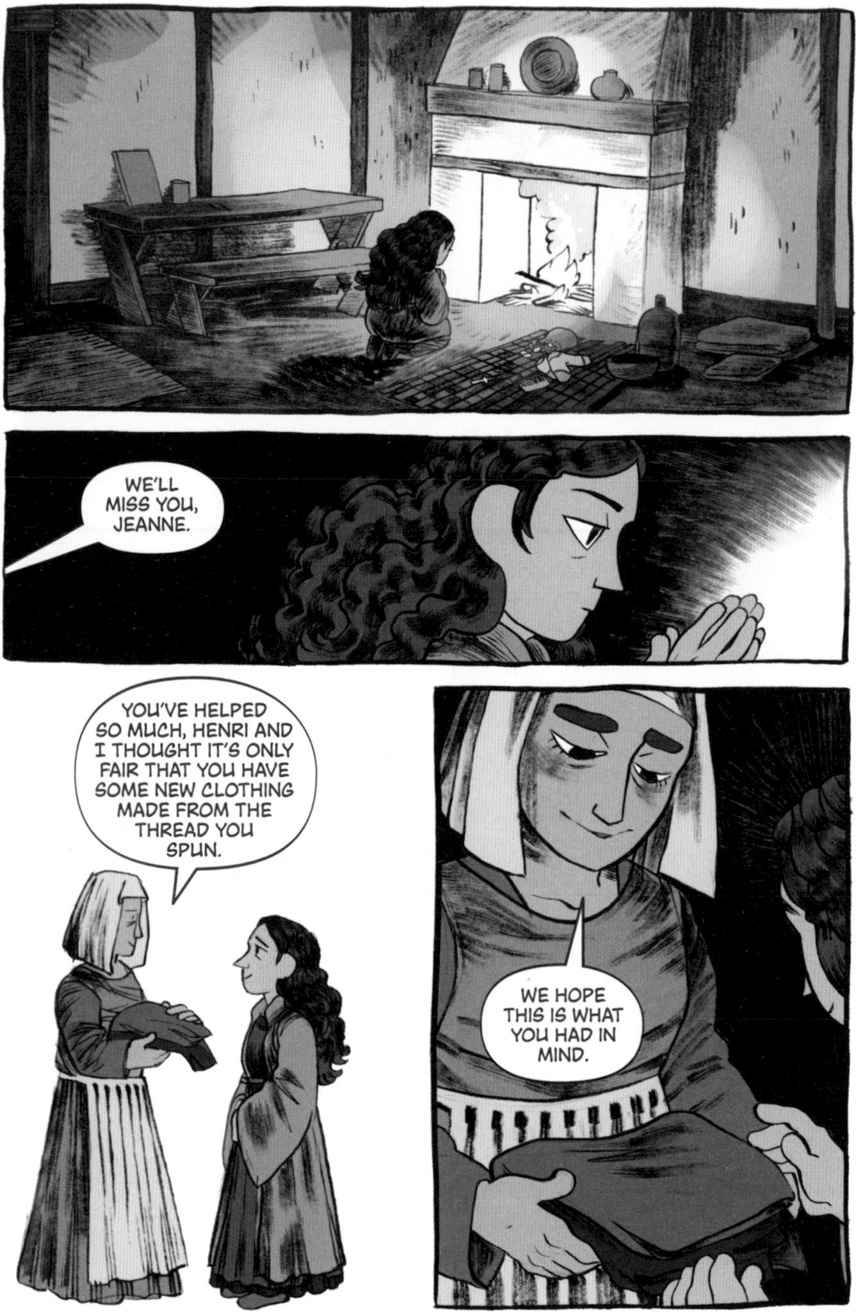
WE'LL MISS YOU, JEANNE.
YOU'VE HELPED SO MUCH, HENRI AND I THOUGHT IT'S ONLY FAIR THAT YOU HAVE SOME NEW CLOTHING MADE FROM THE THREAD YOU SPUN.
WE HOPE THIS IS WHAT YOU HAD IN MIND.

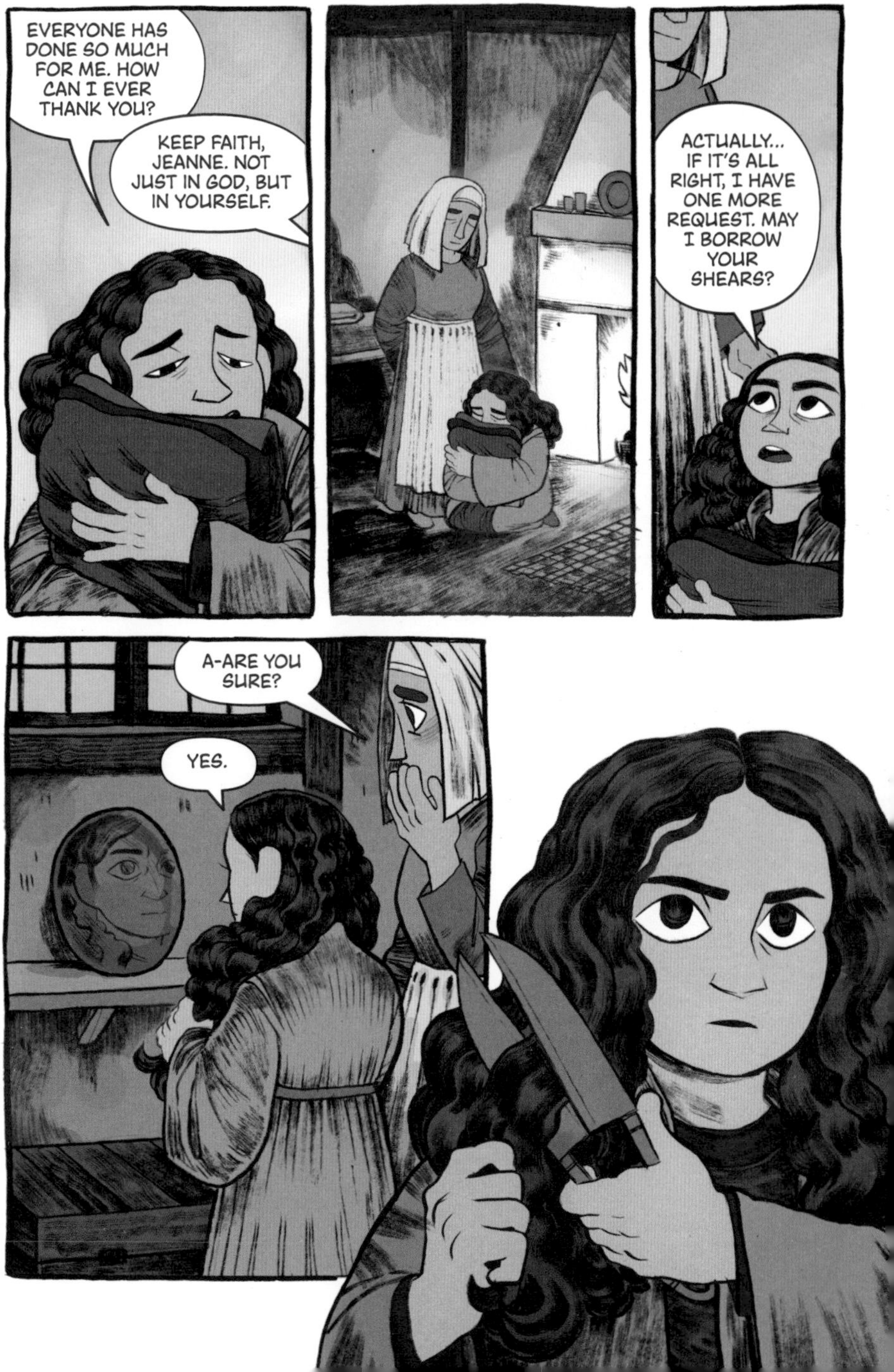
EVERYONE HAS DONE SO MUCH FOR ME. HOW CAN I EVER THANK YOU?
KEEP FAITH, JEANNE. NOT JUST IN GOD, BUT IN YOURSELF.
ACTUALLY... IF IT'S ALL RIGHT, I HAVE ONE MORE REQUEST. MAY I BORROW YOUR SHEARS?
A-ARE YOU SURE?
YES.

Heresy in Catholicism

Heresy is a belief or action that goes against what is accepted in an organized religion. In the fifteenth century, the head of the Catholic Church, the pope, was the most powerful man in Europe, and Catholicism played a big part in shaping laws, governments, and people's daily lives. Anyone who didn't follow the rules of Catholicism was called a heretic, an idea that Jeanne also believed in. At the time, acts of heresy included: questioning Catholic understanding of the Bible; coming up with your own ways to observe holy days; and, sometimes, wearing clothing that didn't match your assigned gender. Heresy was punishable by prison, torture, or even death.

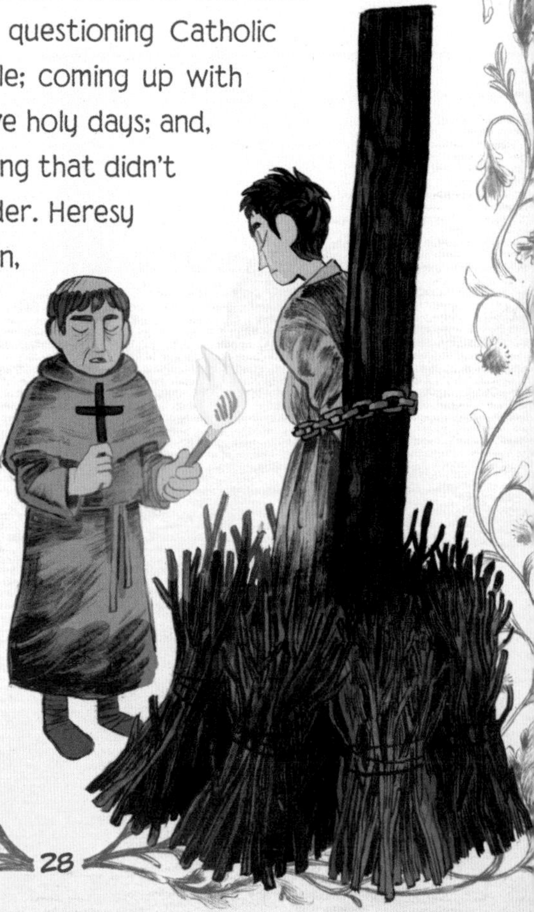

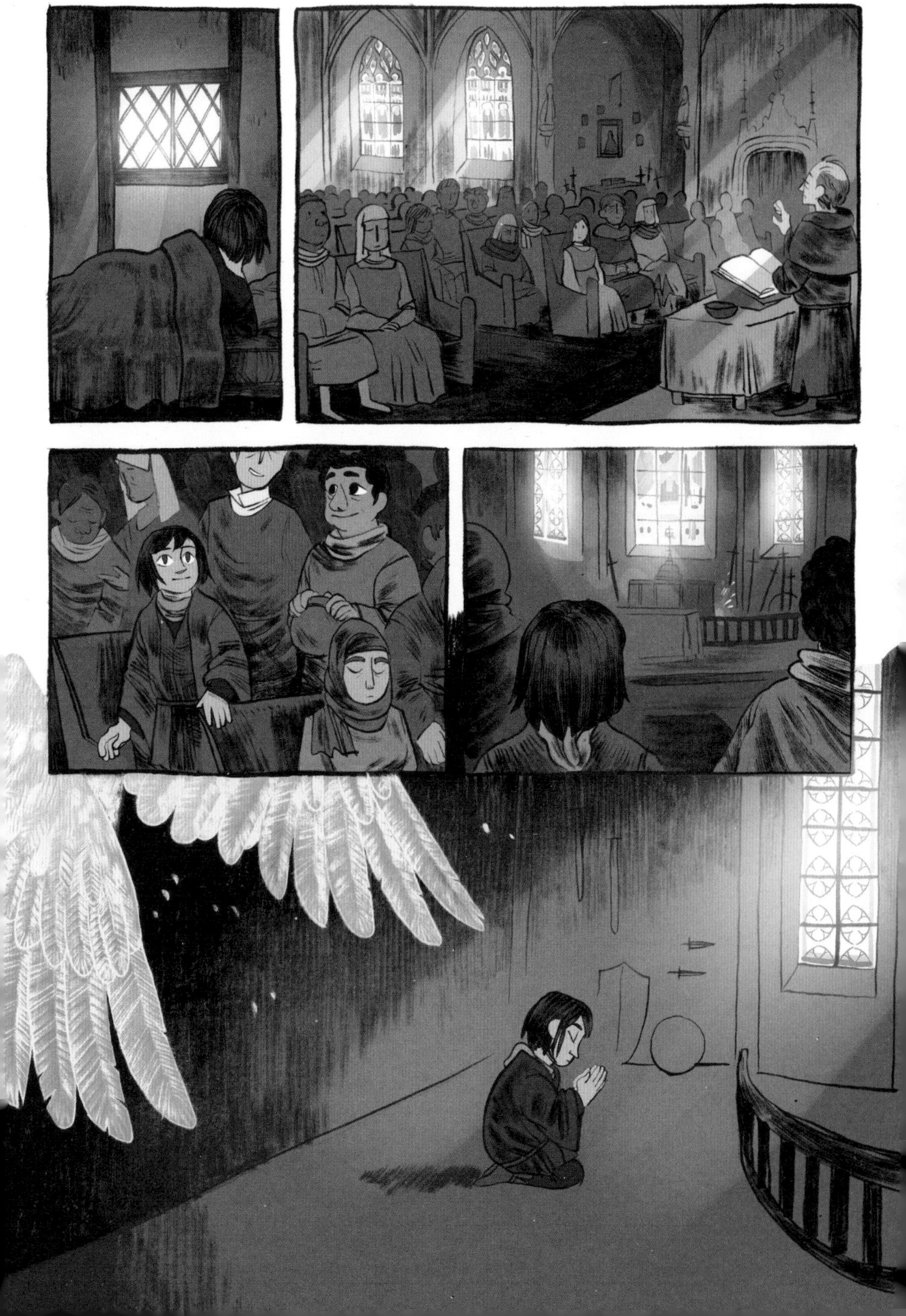

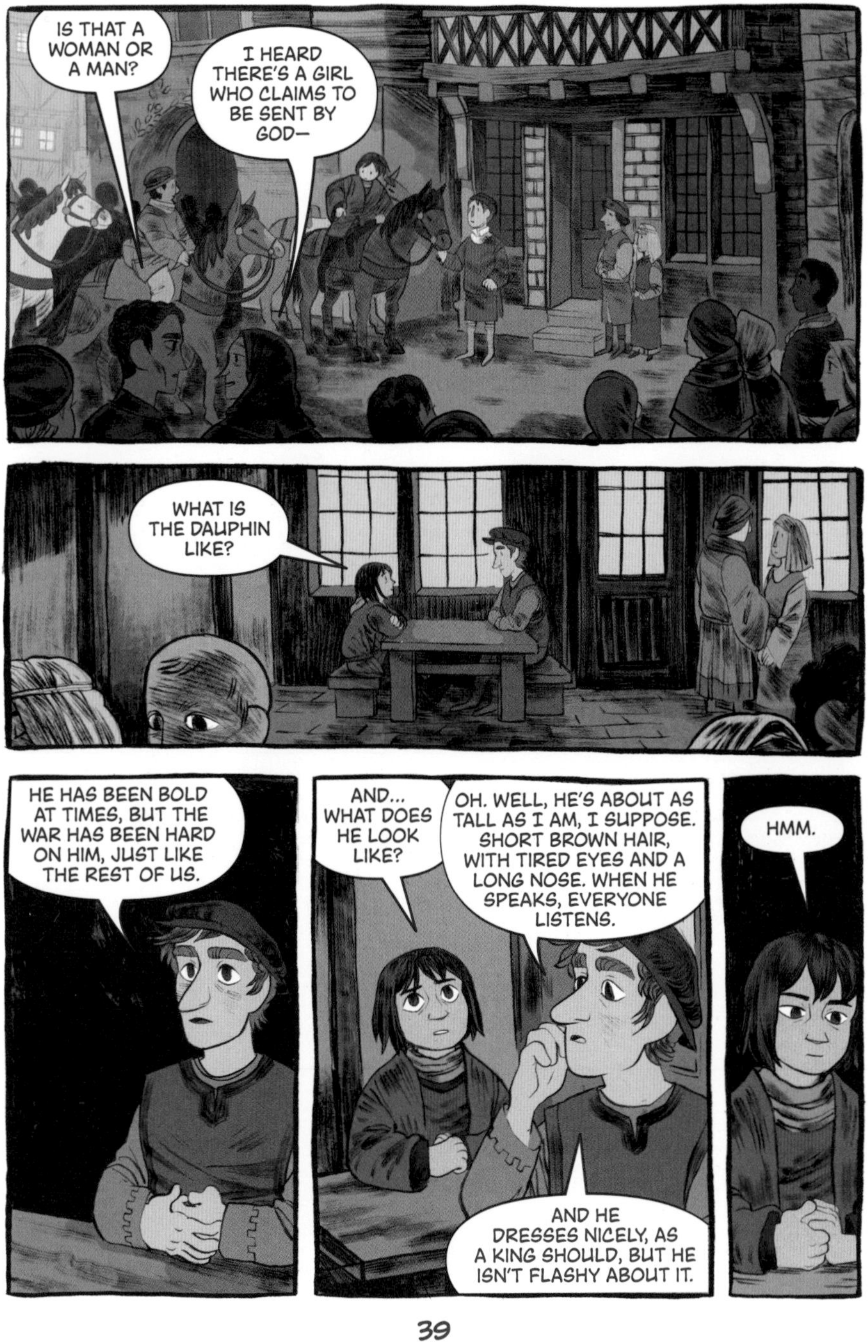
IS THAT A WOMAN OR A MAN?
I HEARD THERE'S A GIRL WHO CLAIMS TO BE SENT BY GOD—
WHAT IS THE DAUPHIN LIKE?
HE HAS BEEN BOLD AT TIMES, BUT THE WAR HAS BEEN HARD ON HIM, JUST LIKE THE REST OF US.
AND... WHAT DOES HE LOOK LIKE?
OH. WELL, HE'S ABOUT AS TALL AS I AM, I SUPPOSE. SHORT BROWN HAIR, WITH TIRED EYES AND A LONG NOSE. WHEN HE SPEAKS, EVERYONE LISTENS.
AND HE DRESSES NICELY, AS A KING SHOULD, BUT HE ISN'T FLASHY ABOUT IT.
HMM.

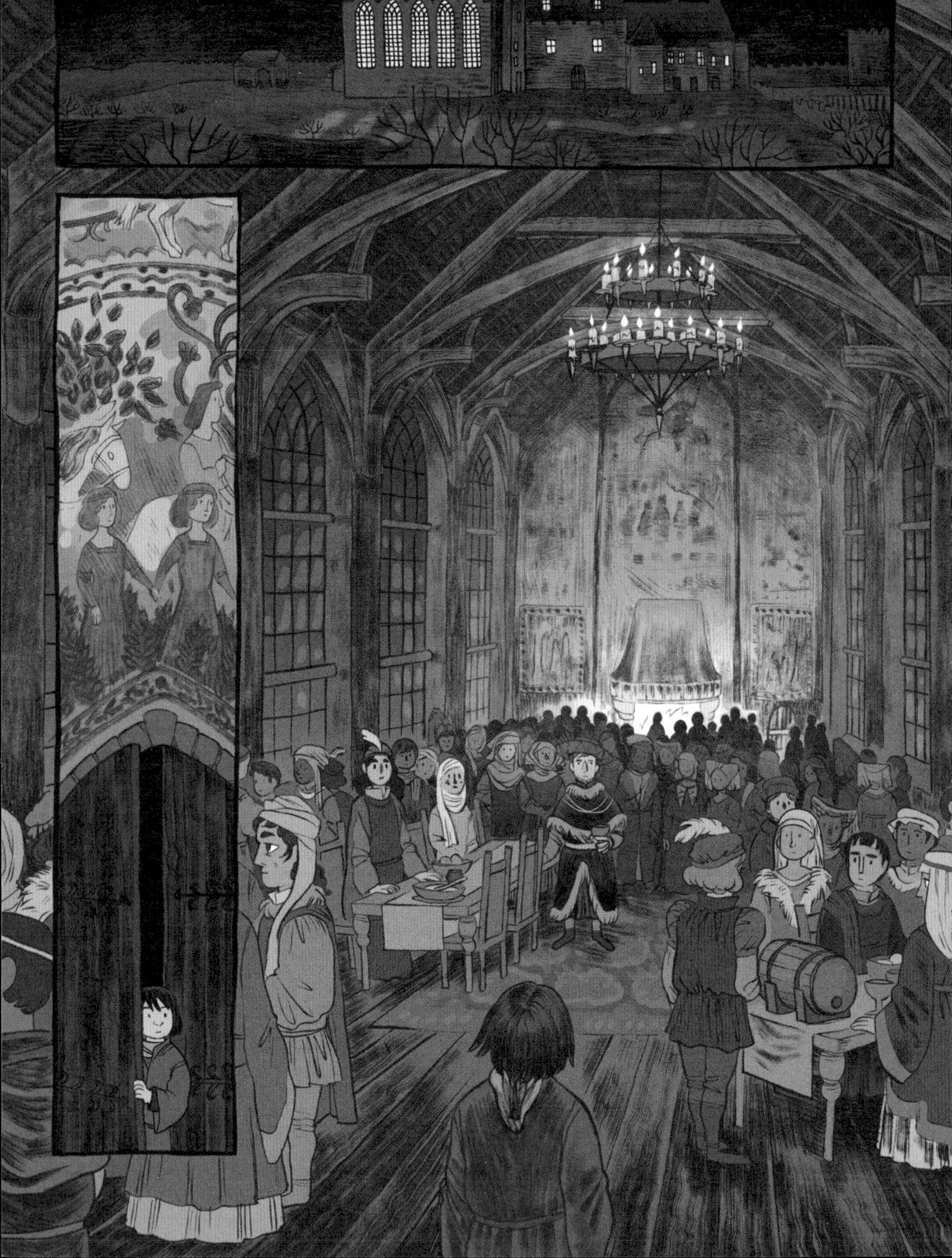

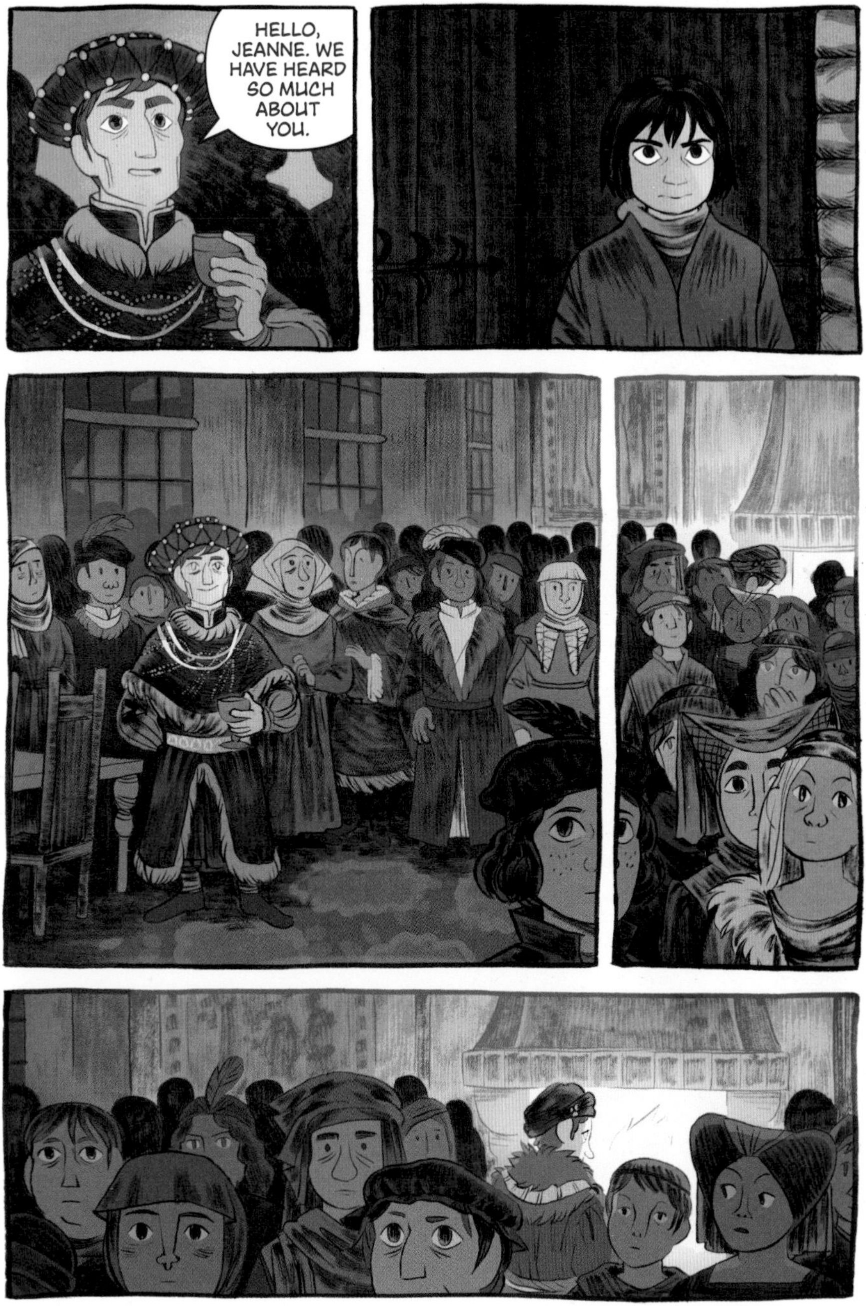
HELLO, JEANNE. WE HAVE HEARD SO MUCH ABOUT YOU.

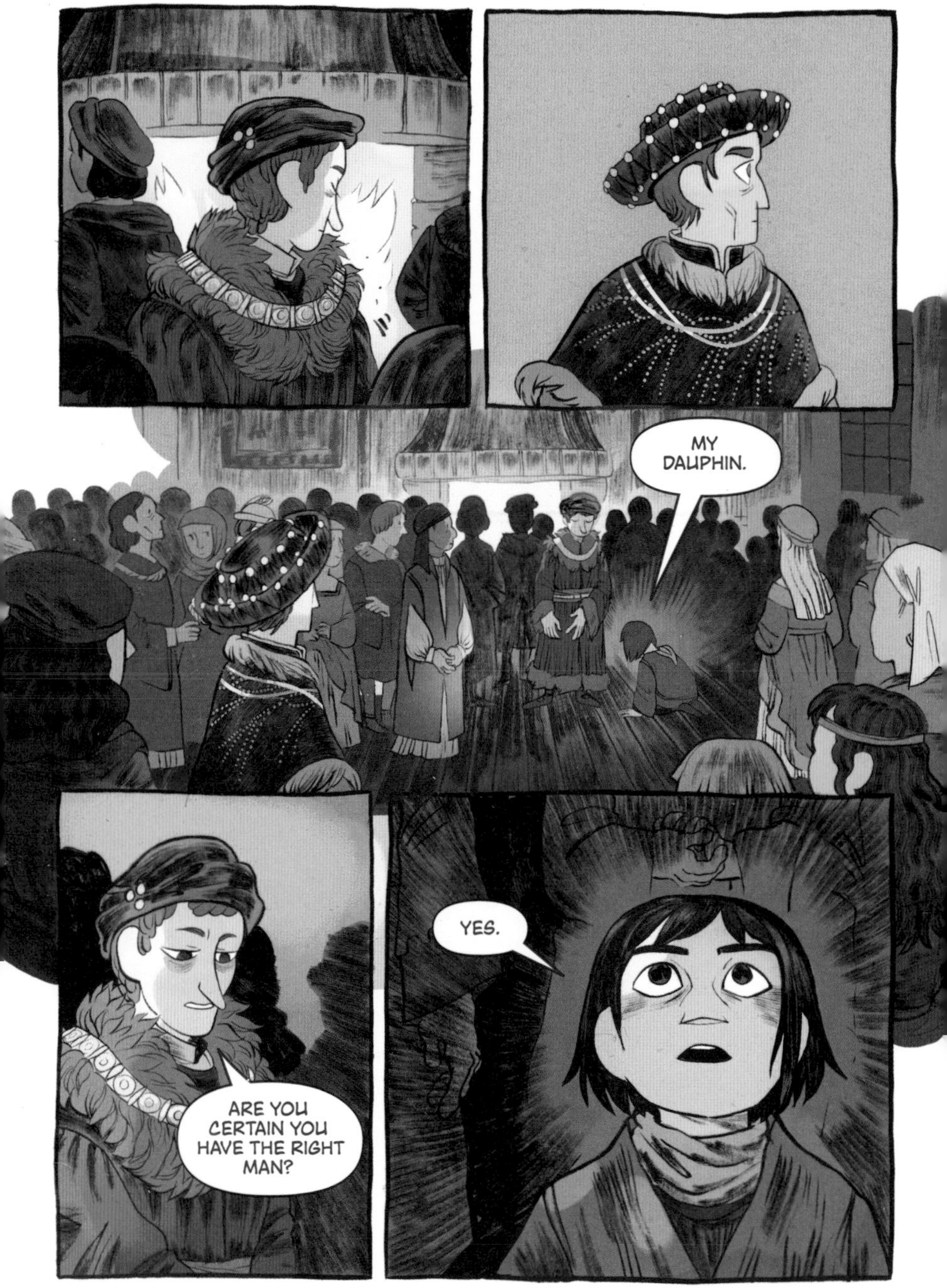
MY DAUPHIN.
ARE YOU CERTAIN YOU HAVE THE RIGHT MAN?
YES.

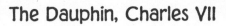

The Dauphin, Charles VII

Born in 1403, Charles VII was the son of Charles VI, who was also known as the mad king of France. Charles VII succeeded in eventually freeing France from English rule in the Hundred Years' War and reestablishing the French monarchy. Before he was crowned king, Charles VII was known as the dauphin, which is a fancy title France gave its first heir to the throne. It means *dolphin* in French, an animal that the first dauphin, Guigues IV, wore on his coat of arms.

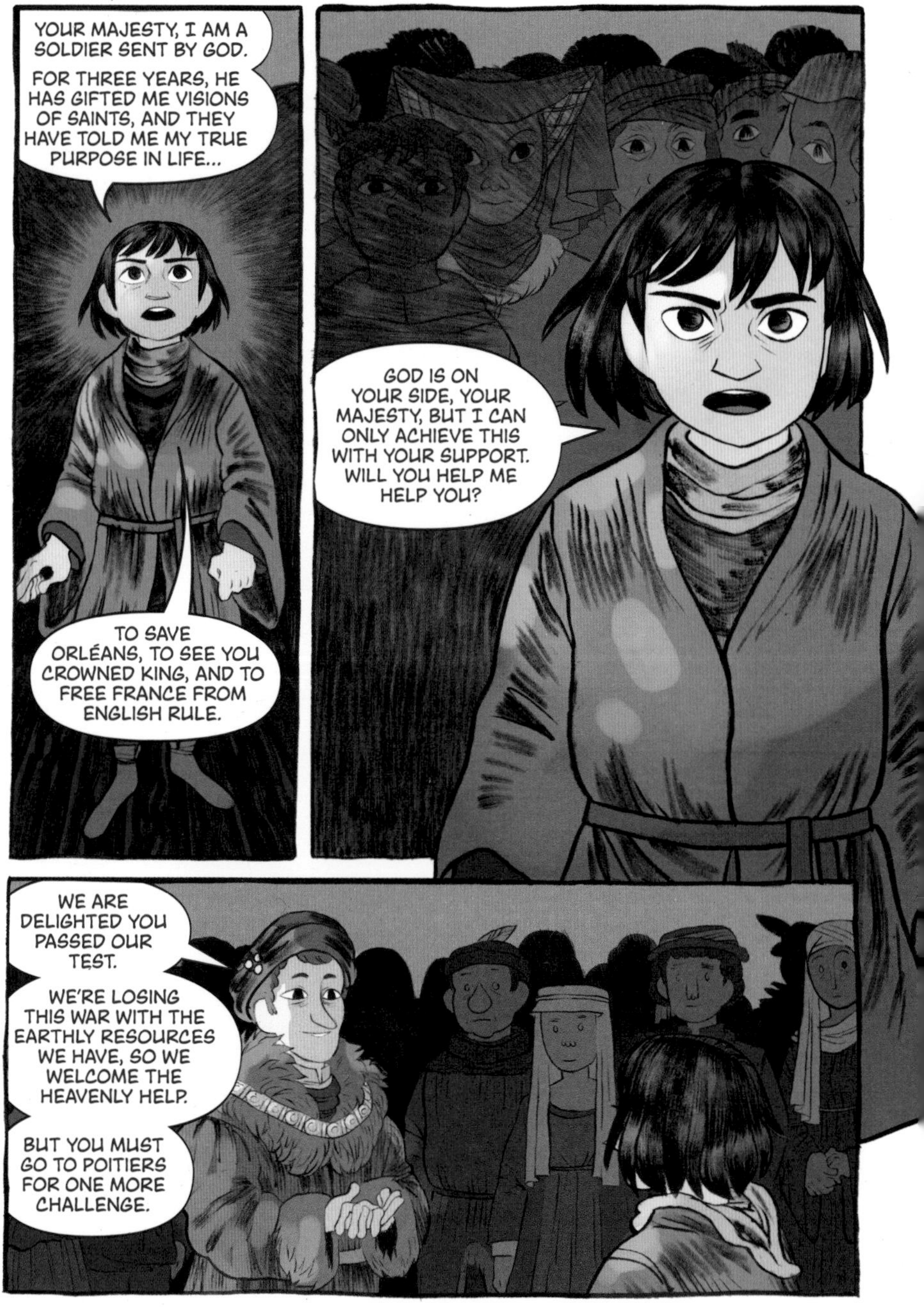
YOUR MAJESTY, I AM A SOLDIER SENT BY GOD.
FOR THREE YEARS, HE HAS GIFTED ME VISIONS OF SAINTS, AND THEY HAVE TOLD ME MY TRUE PURPOSE IN LIFE...
TO SAVE ORLÉANS, TO SEE YOU CROWNED KING, AND TO FREE FRANCE FROM ENGLISH RULE.
GOD IS ON YOUR SIDE, YOUR MAJESTY, BUT I CAN ONLY ACHIEVE THIS WITH YOUR SUPPORT. WILL YOU HELP ME HELP YOU?
WE ARE DELIGHTED YOU PASSED OUR TEST.
WE'RE LOSING THIS WAR WITH THE EARTHLY RESOURCES WE HAVE, SO WE WELCOME THE HEAVENLY HELP.
BUT YOU MUST GO TO POITIERS FOR ONE MORE CHALLENGE.

48

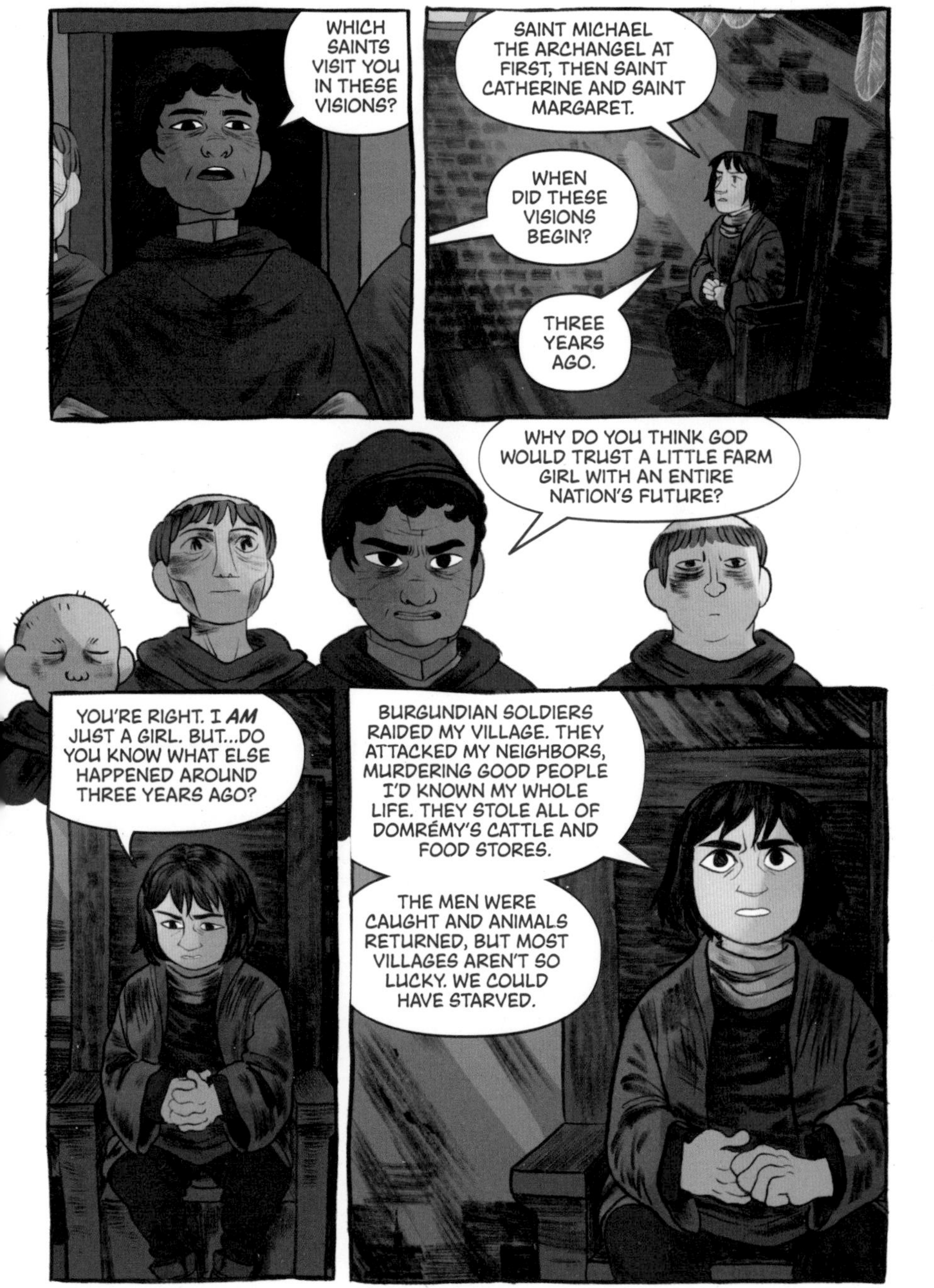
WHICH SAINTS VISIT YOU IN THESE VISIONS?
SAINT MICHAEL THE ARCHANGEL AT FIRST, THEN SAINT CATHERINE AND SAINT MARGARET.
WHEN DID THESE VISIONS BEGIN?
THREE YEARS AGO.
WHY DO YOU THINK GOD WOULD TRUST A LITTLE FARM GIRL WITH AN ENTIRE NATION'S FUTURE?
YOU'RE RIGHT. I *AM* JUST A GIRL. BUT...DO YOU KNOW WHAT ELSE HAPPENED AROUND THREE YEARS AGO?
BURGUNDIAN SOLDIERS RAIDED MY VILLAGE. THEY ATTACKED MY NEIGHBORS, MURDERING GOOD PEOPLE I'D KNOWN MY WHOLE LIFE. THEY STOLE ALL OF DOMRÉMY'S CATTLE AND FOOD STORES.
THE MEN WERE CAUGHT AND ANIMALS RETURNED, BUT MOST VILLAGES AREN'T SO LUCKY. WE COULD HAVE STARVED.

Sainthood

In the Catholic religion, saints are people who led good Christian lives and are thought to have a very close relationship to God. Only the leader of the Catholic Church, the pope, can decide to grant them sainthood. After a person dies, high-ranking Catholic officials gather proof to see if this person has lived a holy life. They also try to find proof that the person has a caused a miracle after their death—a process called beatification. But there is one exception: A martyr, someone who has died for their beliefs, can be beatified without a proven miracle.

Once these people become official saints, living Catholics look to them as role models.

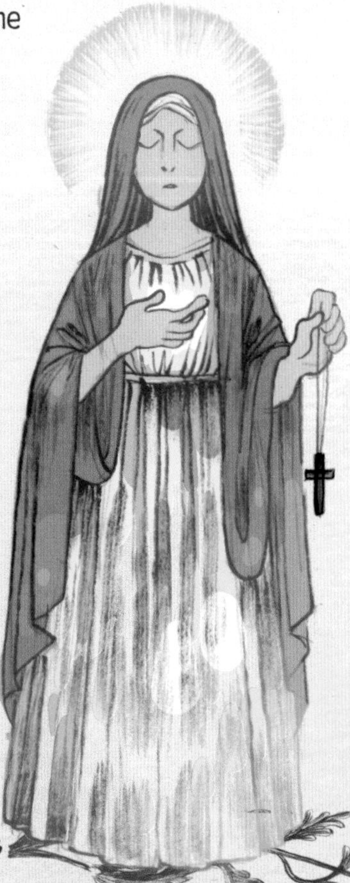

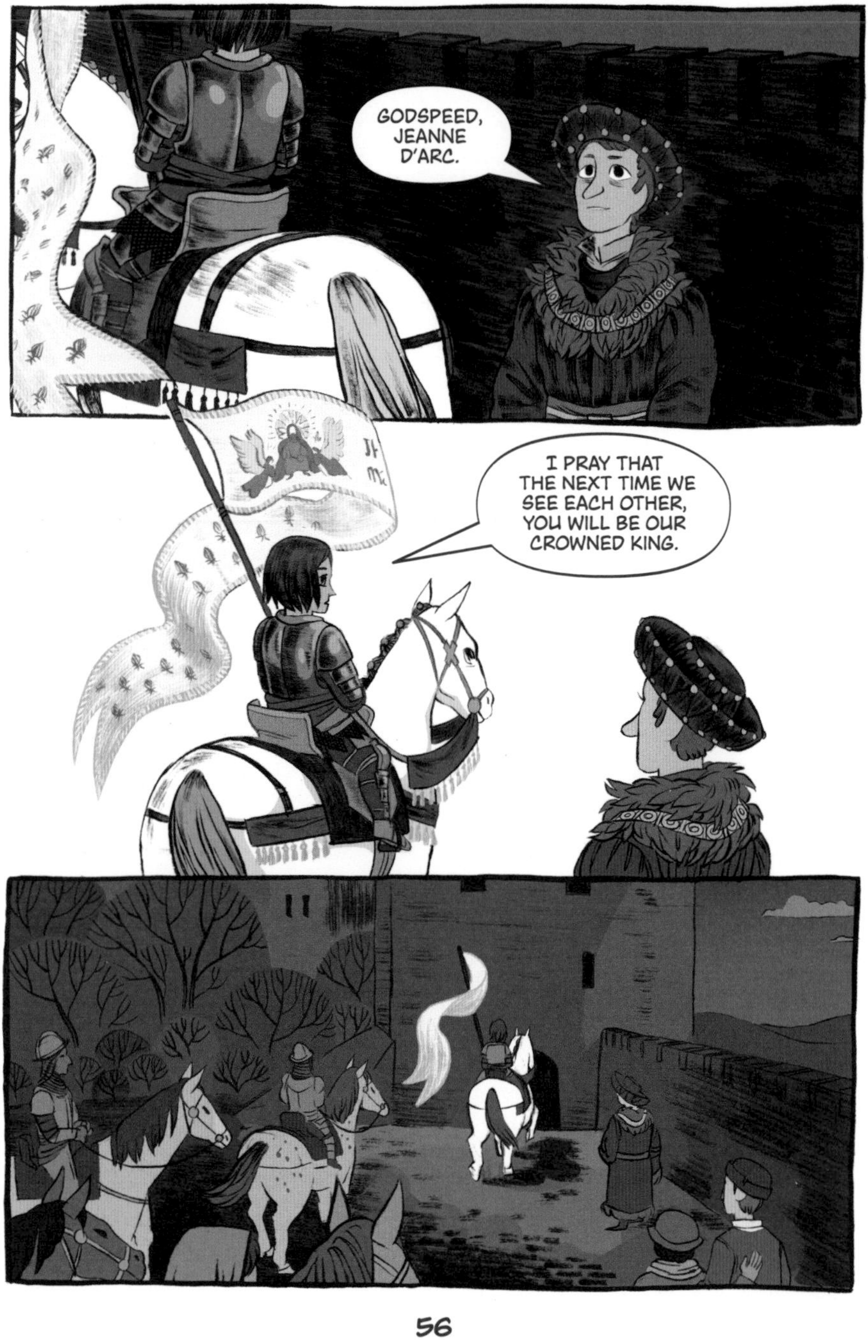
GODSPEED, JEANNE D'ARC.
I PRAY THAT THE NEXT TIME WE SEE EACH OTHER, YOU WILL BE OUR CROWNED KING.

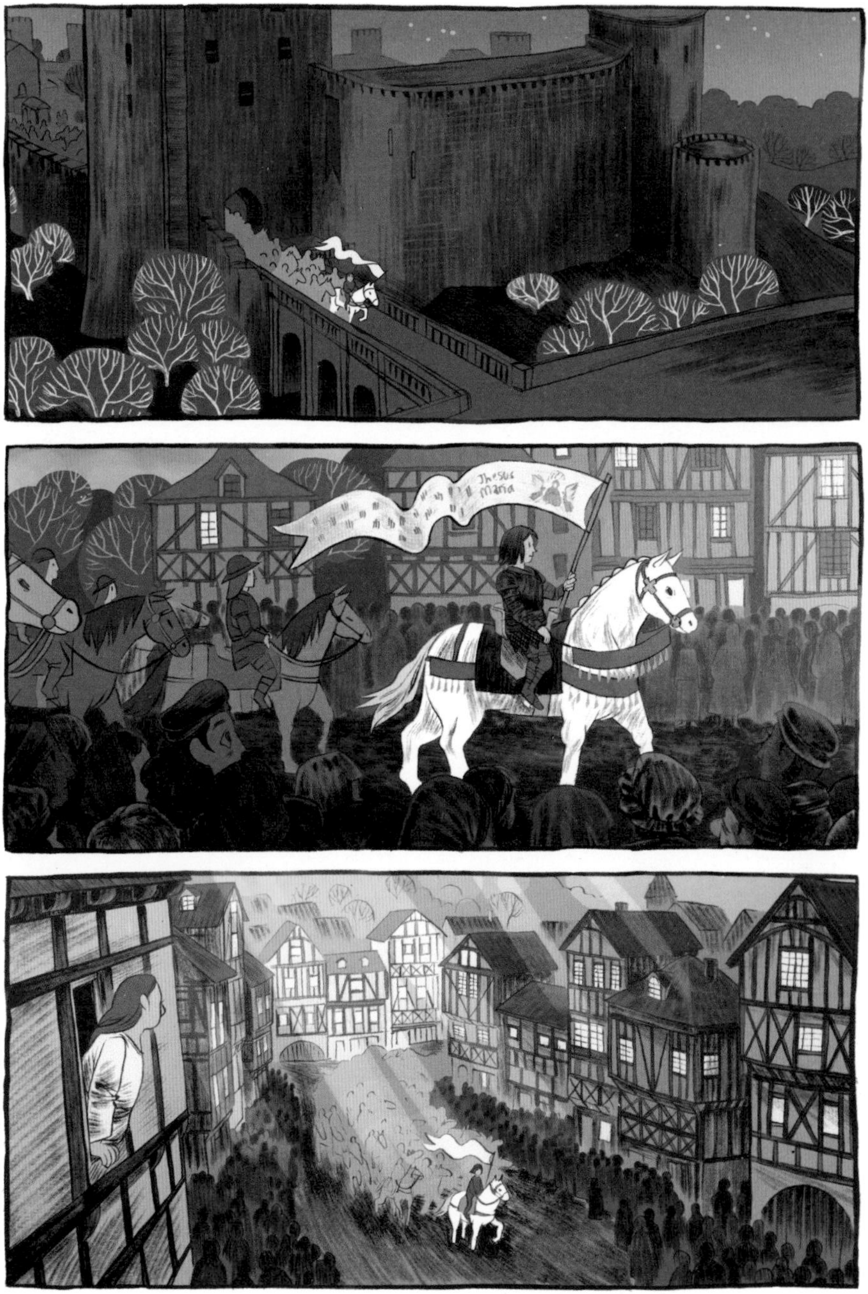
Jhesus Maria

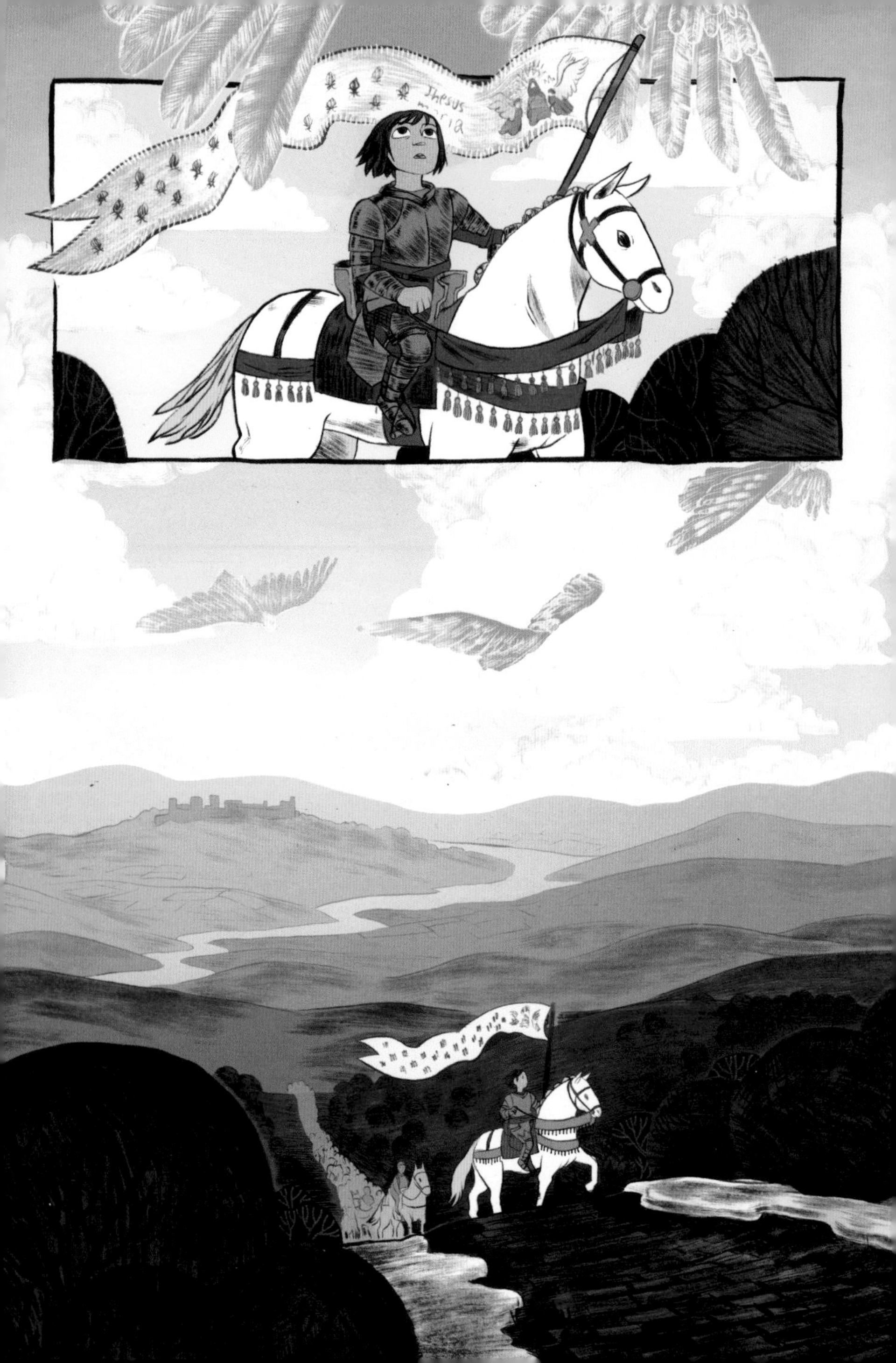
Jhesus
maria

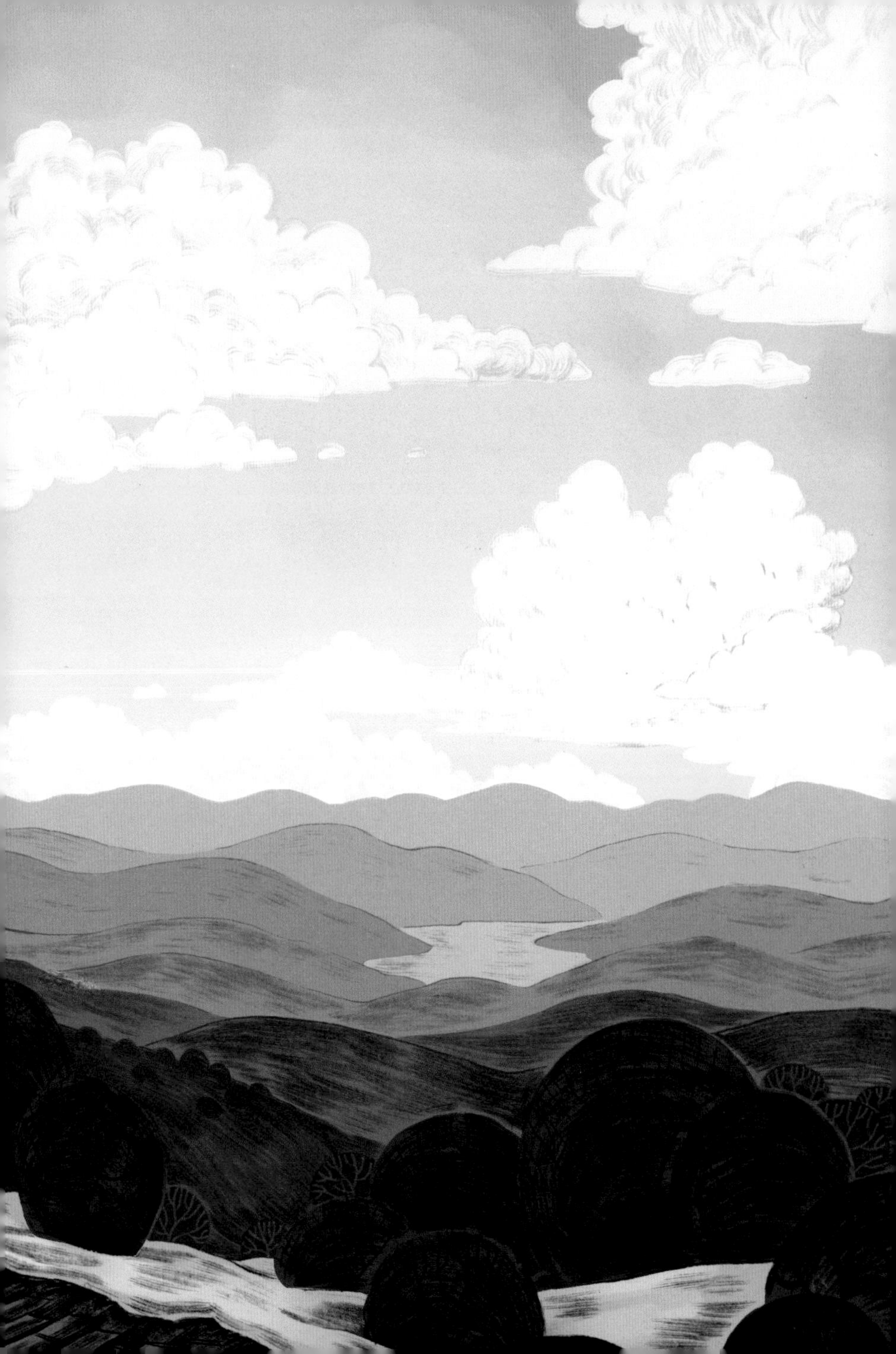

Conclusion

And so Jeanne rode to Orléans, bringing the last hope of France's freedom with her. Together with the rest of the army, she pushed English forces out of the city and saw the dauphin crowned as King Charles VII. Jeanne never used her sword to hurt another person, but she carried her banner into many battles in the Hundred Years' War and inspired France's people along the way.

England didn't like that France started winning battles again all of a sudden. The English were also Catholic and wanted to believe that God was on their side, too. So they decided what must have happened: Jeanne wasn't sent by God at all, and instead, she got her power from the Devil. It couldn't possibly be that God had abandoned them.

In May 1430, Burgundian soldiers captured Jeanne. She tried to escape their castle, but it was no use. Burgundy sold her to England, who held a trial for the heresy they thought she had committed. Jeanne explained that, with God's blessing, she wore men's clothes in order to protect herself. They still found her guilty, and Jeanne died from execution by burning in May 1431.

After Jeanne's death, Charles VII used her victories to pave the rest of the way to freedom. He gradually drove all the English invaders out of France and finally ended the war. Jeanne's mother,

Isabelle, fought her own battle, working hard until the Catholic Church cleared Jeanne's name of heresy and declared her a martyr. Today, Jeanne is an official patron saint of France.

Religion and politics were impossible to separate in Jeanne's time, which makes her story complicated. It is true that Jeanne helped end a terrible war. But it is also true that she promoted violence against people just for having different religious beliefs. Today, she has become a legend for both her spiritual and historical contributions. Her story has gone on to change the course of France's history forever.

Timeline of Jeanne's Life

c. 1412 — Jeanne is born

1425 — Domrémy is raided, and Jeanne sees her first vision

1428 — Jeanne first visits Vaucouleurs to request Robert de Baudricourt's assistance, and he says no

— Domrémy is raided again and burned

1429 — In January, Jeanne returns to Vaucouleurs to ask for Baudricourt's help again, but this time she finds more support

— In February, the Battle of the Herrings sees France lose outside Orléans; Jeanne's prediction comes true, and Baudricourt finally agrees to help her

— In March, Jeanne meets the dauphin in Chinon

— In April, Jeanne reaches Orléans to join the fight

— In July, the dauphin is officially crowned as Charles VII, King of France

1430 — Burgundian soldiers capture Jeanne

1431 — Jeanne dies by execution after English courts find her guilty of heresy

1456 — Declared a martyr, Jeanne is cleared as innocent

1920 — The Catholic Church grants Jeanne d'Arc sainthood

Bibliography

*Books for young readers

*Brooks, Polly Schoyer. *Beyond the Myth: The Story of Joan of Arc.* Boston: HMH Books for Young Readers, 1999.

Meissonier, Martin, dir. *The Real Joan of Arc.* Arte France Productions, 2007. Amazon Prime Video.

Pernoud, Régine, and Marie-Véronique Clin. *Joan of Arc: Her Story.* Translated by Jeremy DuQuesnay Adams. New York: St. Martin's Griffin, 1999.

*Pollack, Pam, and Meg Belviso. *Who Was Joan of Arc?* New York: Penguin Workshop, 2016.

*Stanley, Diane. *Joan of Arc.* New York: HarperCollins, 2002.

*Wilkinson, Philip. *Joan of Arc: The Teenager Who Saved Her Nation.* Washington, DC: National Geographic Children's Books, 2009.

Sarah Winifred Searle

originally hails from spooky New England but currently lives in sunny Perth, Australia. She writes and draws comics for all sorts of audiences, best known for vulnerable memoir and compassionate fiction. Find her around the web: @swinsea / swinsea.com.

Maria Capelle Frantz

was born and raised in Fairbanks, Alaska, where she spent the first years of her life playing in the woods, making up stories, and regularly perusing the local comic shop. In 2015, she was awarded a national gold medal in the Scholastic Art and Writing Awards for her short comic "Death Wish." Her debut graphic novel, *The Chancellor and the Citadel*, was published by Iron Circus Comics in January 2019. Find her on Instagram and Twitter: @mariacfrantz.